CONTENT

CHAPTER 1

'Come on, all you lazy boys and girls! Get up! Look outside – it's a sunny day again! It's eight o'clock on this super Sunday morning. It's going to be as hot as the music here on Radio Chester, but don't forget, it could be rainy in the afternoon. And now a song for everybody in bed. It's the Small Faces with "Lazy Sunday".'

Mrs Payne looked out of the kitchen window. She saw Terry. He was in the Paynes' garden. These hot summer days weren't easy for an old dog like him. This was the third hot week in July. It was too hot for people and animals. Terry was lying under a big apple tree. He liked this tree. He always slept a little there in the afternoon. And on a warm morning like this it was cool under the tree. From the green grass under the tree Terry could watch HIM – Boris, of course! He often ran after the

neighbours' cat – it was good fun. Terry looked at the Kellys' house, but there was no Boris and there were no Kellys. They were all still in bed. Time to get up, Kelly-cat!

Mrs Payne listened to the music on the radio. She was going to cook bacon and eggs with sausages for Sunday breakfast.

'Good morning, Helen.'

Suddenly Mrs Payne's face was wet. What was that? It was Mr Payne's face. Mrs Payne looked at Mr Payne. There was lots of shaving foam on Mr Payne's face.

'Oh George. Please, stop it! I thought it was Terry's nose.'

'What? Terry? Can Terry talk? Can he be in two places at the same time? Look, there he is, under the tree!' Mr Payne laughed. 'Soon he's going to have his own TV programme with all his tricks. Is the Sunday newspaper here?'

'Oh, George! The newspaper! I forgot about it! Well, that's Terry's job,' Mrs Payne said. I'm going to fetch Terry's plastic bag.'

'OK! I'm going to go upstairs and tell Sharon, Luke and Kevin that it's time to get up.'

Mr Payne left the kitchen and went upstairs to the children's bedrooms. 'Time to get up, everybody,' he shouted before he went into the bathroom.

'Terry! Come here!' Mrs Payne shouted.

When Terry saw the plastic bag for the newspaper, his face said: No! Not today! – But what was that in Mrs Payne's left hand? Wasn't that a sausage? Oh, OK! I can go and fetch the newspaper for you.

'You look great, Terry! Like a shopping bag with four legs,' Mrs Payne smiled.

Terry was only interested in his sausage. A few minutes later he ran down Elm Road. There was no sign of Boris.

'Where are the new videos?' Mr Ahmed asked Asif who always helped his father in the shop on Sundays. Then Mr Ahmed saw Terry.

'You're late, Terry,' Mr Ahmed smiled. 'It's too hot for two old men like us!'

What a friendly man this shopkeeper was!

'The Sunday newspaper for the Paynes just like every Sunday.'

Mr Ahmed put it into Terry's plastic bag.

'And here's a chocolate for you, Terry,' said Asif, and he gave Terry a chocolate. Well, a sausage and a chocolate – not bad for a Sunday breakfast.

CHAPTER 2

The Paynes were sitting at the kitchen table.

'I'm so hungry, Mum,' Kevin said.

'Breakfast is going to be ready soon,' Mrs Payne answered.

'And what are you planning for today?' Mr Payne asked. 'You know that your mum and I are going to Liverpool today. We're going to visit your grandmother in hospital.'

'I think I'm going to have a lazy Sunday, Dad,' Luke said and poured some milk into his glass.

'I'm going to the swimming pool with Bina and Claire. We're going to meet at two o'clock at the Kellys' house,' Sharon said. 'Can I have two eggs with my bacon, Mum?'

'Can I come with you?' Luke asked.

'I'm sorry. Girls only!' Sharon smiled.

Silly girls! Luke was angry.

'I think it's a nice day for a picnic in the park, Luke. You have to look after your brother today. You know that your father and I are going to be back very late.'

'Why can't Sharon look after him? She's older than I am,' Luke asked.

'Don't be angry,' Mr Payne said. 'You have to help us, Luke. You can feed the birds, play football and lie next to the lake. And you can have an ice-cream!'

'An ice-cream! I want an ice-cream now!' Kevin shouted with a big smile on his face.

'No. Not now. Later,' said Mr Payne.

'That's a good idea, Dad,' Luke said. But he wasn't very happy. 'Let's have a lazy Sunday in the park, Kevin.'

Luke and Kevin put some rolls, some fruit and some cans of cola into a picnic bag. Then Kevin saw Terry in front of the garden gate. He opened the kitchen door and ran to Terry. He took Terry's bag with the newspaper in it.

'Terry the superdog!' Sharon laughed and stroked her dog. 'Here's your favourite toy bone, Terry,' Sharon said. But Terry wasn't interested. He ran out of the kitchen. A moment later he was at the apple tree. Terry barked and then he ran into the Kellys' garden.

'Boris is in the garden!' Sharon explained.

'A game with Boris and then a walk to the park! That's too much for an old dog like Terry,' Luke smiled.

'I hope that he's going to bring some flowers for your grandmother from the Kellys' garden,' Mr Payne said.

Everybody laughed.

CHAPTER 3

After breakfast Mr and Mrs Payne got in the car and drove to Liverpool.

Sharon went to the Kellys' house. She had fun with Bina and Claire, and then they went to the swimming pool.

Terry was under the big apple tree in the Paynes' garden. He was having a dream. In his dream there were no flowers in the flower-bed, only very big sausages.

'Come on, Terry! Get up! It's time to go!'

Terry opened his eyes and saw Luke and Kevin – and a big picnic bag with lots of food and two big sausages.

'Let's go and have a nice picnic in the park,' Luke said.

The two boys went to the garden gate and waited for Terry. Terry closed his eyes again.

'Terry!' Luke shouted. 'Aren't you coming? Oh, well. If you don't want your sausages, we can give them to Boris.'

Oh no! I don't like that idea. OK! You win! I'm coming!

Terry walked along the green grass and followed Luke and Kevin. He looked behind and saw Mr Kelly in his garden. He was watering the flower-beds. There was no sign of Boris. Poor cat! He was frightened of water.

Luke, Kevin and Terry went down Elm Road. Then they turned into London Road. They saw Mr and Mrs Ahmed's shop. There were a lot of customers in the shop now. Then they walked into the city centre. In Chester's main shopping street Luke put down the picnic bag in front of a sports shop.

'It's so hot, Kevin,' he said. 'Let's have our picnic here and open the first can of cola.'

Kevin laughed. 'I want to go to the park and have an ice-cream.'

Luke looked at the sports clothes in the shop window. 'Look at those trainers, Kevin,' Luke said.

'Black and yellow – I like the colours,' Kevin answered.

'But look how expensive they are.'

'£35,' Kevin read. 'Well, don't buy so many hamburgers, Luke. Then you can buy the trainers.'

'You must be joking, Kevin. Don't forget that I gave you £3 for the cinema last Saturday!'

There was no answer.

'Kevin! Kevin?'

Luke turned round. Kevin wasn't there. Then he saw Kevin and Terry. They were in front of the north gate of Chester Park.

CHAPTER 4

'Let's stay here, Kevin. It's a nice place, and we're under a big tree.'

'I'm thirsty. Can I have a drink?'

Luke opened the picnic bag. There was a blanket and a ball in it. And there were two cans of cola, two cans of lemonade, four rolls with cheese, two eggs, three apples, two bananas and two sausages for Terry.

'It's two o'clock,' Luke said. 'It's early in the afternoon, but there are lots of people in the park.'

'It's fun to watch them,' Kevin said. 'It's like a big party in the park.'

Some men were sleeping on their blankets under big trees. Some women were lying in the sun. Other people were reading books or listening to the music on Radio Chester. A few families were having lunch. Some children were playing 'hide-and-seek' behind the trees and the bushes. Other boys and girls were playing with a ball.

'Look at Terry! He likes the park, too,' Kevin said. 'He's playing with a poodle, and he isn't tired.' Then Kevin took a can of cola and drank a little.

'The apples are great,' Luke said. 'They're from the apple tree in our garden.'

Suddenly Mrs Kelly was in front of them.

'Hallo, boys! Nice to see you. Where are the other Paynes, or is it a boys' party today?' Mrs Kelly smiled.

'Oh no, Mrs Kelly,' Luke said. 'Mum and dad are in

Liverpool today. They're going to visit grandma. She's in hospital.'

'Oh no, that's a pity. I hope your grandma is going to get better soon. I like her a lot. She always tells great jokes. Is she over eighty years old now?'

'Yes, and she's going to live forever,' Kevin answered.

They all laughed.

'Where's Sharon?' asked Luke.

'She's at the swimming pool with Bina and Claire. I must buy some food for the girls. I'm sure that they're going to be very hungry when they come back. But tell me – where's your monster dog?'

'Who? Terry? He's with us, but I can't see him,' Luke answered.

Luke was worried. There were too many people, too many dogs, too many trees and too many bushes in the park. He couldn't see Terry. Then suddenly he heard Terry's bark.

'There he is! There's Terry!' Kevin shouted. 'He's with two other dogs. They're running after a tennis ball.'

'Well, have a nice picnic, boys,' Mrs Kelly said.

'Bye, Mrs Kelly.'

Luke and Kevin ate a cheese roll and drank a can of lemonade. Then they played ball. It was very hot, and Kevin wasn't very good. But Luke wasn't angry with him.

Suddenly there was somebody behind Luke.

'Look, it's the two football champions!'

Luke turned round and saw Hanif. Hanif was in Luke's class. PE was Hanif's favourite subject at school and he played football a lot. He was much better than Luke at football.

'Hallo Hanif! Do you want to play with us?'

'I'm sorry, Luke. I can't. I have to go home. My dad is

waiting for the Sunday paper. I went out to buy it for him. He always reads the sports pages on Sunday. His favourite football club is ...'

Suddenly there was a thunderclap. It was far away, but it was cloudy now over the park. Then the lightning came.

'Oh no, I think that it's going to rain,' Hanif said. 'I'm going home. Bye!'

Hanif ran to the gate of the park. Kevin was frightened.

'Let's go home,' he said.

'Don't worry, Kevin. The lightning is far away. And what about our ice-creams?'

'I don't want an ice-cream now. I don't want to get wet.'

Luke put the blanket and the ball into the picnic bag, and he put the empty cans into the bin. Then he felt the first raindrops on his arms.

What a funny park! Everybody was running – old women and young men, and children and dogs ... Dogs! Where was Terry? Was he still playing with the other dogs? Luke couldn't see them.

'I have to look for Terry, Kevin. Stay here. I'm going to run to the bushes over there,' Luke explained. He was worried and angry. Luke looked and looked.

'Terry! Terry!' he shouted. It was raining a lot now.

More and more people left the park. Again and again Luke shouted Terry's name. He listened. But Terry didn't bark. He only heard the rain and the thunder.

'I'm sure that Terry went home,' Luke said when he came back to his brother. 'He's a clever dog. He hates thunderstorms – just like you, Kevin.'

The two boys didn't smile.

'Look how wet I am, Luke. It's so windy. Let's run home.'

CHAPTER 5

'Luke, wait for me!'

But Luke didn't listen to his brother. He ran very fast.

'Please, Terry. Be under the apple tree or in front of the door,' Luke thought.

The two boys were in Elm Road now. They were very wet. It was half past four in the afternoon, but it was dark. There was a big thunderstorm over Chester. Luke could see the garden gate now. Here were the flower-beds, and there was the green grass with the apple tree. Luke looked left and right, but there was no Terry. There was only the Paynes' house. Luke was sad. He closed his eyes. A moment later Kevin arrived at the house. He looked at Luke and knew the answer to his question. They went into the house. They were very wet and very sad.

'What are mum and dad going to say? And Sharon?! It's our fault,' Kevin said.

'Don't worry, Kevin. A lot of dogs run away and come back the next day.' Luke didn't really believe this. They went upstairs and put on dry clothes.

Half an hour later the two boys were in the living-room. They were watching cartoons on TV. Usually they liked cartoons. But today they couldn't laugh. They were too sad.

Suddenly there was somebody at the door. It was Sharon.

'Hi boys! Gosh, it's raining cats and dogs! But we were lucky. Mr Kelly took us home in his car. What about you? Did you get "wet wet wet"? Do you want to be the new boys' group with the monster dog.'

But Luke and Kevin were quiet.

'Luke, Kevin, what happened? You're so quiet. How was your picnic?'

'Terry is missing,' Luke said. He didn't look at Sharon. 'We don't know where he is.'

Sharon dropped her bag. She sat down on the sofa. Suddenly she felt tired. She didn't understand. Then Luke and Kevin told their story.

'It's all your fault, Luke. You didn't look after Terry! I'm so angry,' Sharon said with tears in her eyes.

Then they were all quiet. The two boys waited.

'OK. Let's think,' Sharon said after a long time. 'Where can Terry be? Do you have an idea?'

'We can go back to the park and look for Terry,' said Luke.

Kevin said, 'I'm sure that he can't find the house. Perhaps he's still in the park.'

They looked out of the window.

'There's still too much rain. I can't even see the Kellys' house. I don't think that that's a good idea,' Sharon said. 'Let's wait here. Terry is a clever dog. He's having a day out. That's all. He's going to be back soon.' The two boys nodded their heads.

'Aren't you hungry? Well, I am,' Sharon said.

She went into the kitchen and took a roll out of the picnic bag. Then she went upstairs to her bedroom.

Sharon had homework, but she couldn't work. She looked at Terry's photos on the wall. She felt sad. Sharon looked at the clock. It was half past seven.

'Mum and dad are back!' Kevin shouted from the living-room.

She ran to the window and saw her parents' car in front of

the house. When she got to the front door, her parents were there.

'What a terrible trip!' Mr Payne said. 'Our car was like a boat on the River Mersey.'

'Can't you swim, Dad?' Luke asked.

Mr and Mrs Payne laughed.

'Grandma feels much better, but she has to stay in hospital for two more weeks. We're all going to visit her next Sunday – with Terry, of course.'

There was no hooray. It was quiet in the living-room.

'Hey, what's the matter? A trip to Liverpool. Don't you like the idea?' Mrs Payne asked.

'Terry is missing,' Sharon said. 'It happened in the park. The rain. The thunderstorm. Luke and Kevin couldn't find him.' Sharon was sad.

'Don't worry, Sharon.' Mrs Payne put her arms around her daughter.

'Please don't worry. He's going to be back soon. He knows where we live,' Mr Payne said and smiled at Sharon.

'Luke and Kevin feel bad. They weren't careful enough,' Sharon said.

A few minutes later the Payne family were sitting at the kitchen table.

'Here are some crisps. I'm sure that you're all hungry,' Mrs Payne said.

'I have an idea,' Mr Payne said and took some crisps. 'It isn't raining now. Sharon and I can go back to the park. Do you have a torch, boys?'

'I have a new torch, Dad,' Kevin said.

'You can have my torch, too. Two torches are better than one. You can see better,' Luke explained.

'Good idea, Luke. You and Kevin talk to the neighbours. First ask the Kellys. Perhaps they know where Terry is.'

'OK, Dad.'

Luke and Kevin felt good. They were helping Sharon and their dad.

At nine o'clock Sharon and her father came back home. Terry wasn't with them. Sharon was tired and sad.

'No luck,' Sharon said. 'It was wet and dark in the park. There was lots of rubbish. But there was no Terry.'

'And what about you, Luke and Kevin? Did you find any new information about Terry?' Mr Payne asked.

'No, we didn't, Dad,' Luke answered. 'The Waltons are on holiday. But the Kellys were at home. They didn't have any information. We met Mrs Kelly in the park this afternoon. But she didn't see Terry when she left the park.'

'What can we do now, Dad?' Sharon asked and looked at her father.

'The animal home!'

'What?'

'Let's not forget the animal home,' Mr Payne said. 'Perhaps somebody found Terry and took him to the animal home. We can go there tomorrow. It's too late to go now. They close at seven o'clock.'

Sharon lay in her bed, but she couldn't sleep. Terry's place by her bed was empty. It was a night of bad dreams.

Terry – where are you?

CHAPTER 6

Chester Animal Home was outside the town. Sharon and her mother went there by car. It was only ten minutes to the animal home by car, but they were ten very long minutes for Sharon. Then she saw a big sign. It was still far away, but Sharon could read the letters of the first word. A-N-I-M-A-L. Then she read the next word. H-O-P-E. H-O-P-E? No, that was wrong. Sharon looked again. Of course, it was H-O-M-E. A good sign? But was there hope behind these walls? Why did people leave their animals alone?

When Sharon got out of the car, she heard a sad noise. Dogs were barking and cats were miaowing – but they weren't happy.

'Hallo, I'm Mrs Potter. What can I do for you?'

Mrs Potter was a nice old woman. Sharon's mother told Terry's story. But Sharon didn't listen. She walked to a cage with some cats in it. There was a black cat – it looked like Boris. How lucky Boris was!

'That's terrible! That's terrible!' Mrs Potter said again and again. 'I can understand why you are very worried.'

'How many animals are there at the animal home, Mrs Potter?' Sharon asked.

'Well, too many, too many, my dear. We have 15 dogs, 12 cats, some birds and a hamster, too. Animals are like toys for some people, you know, my dear. It's so sad.' Mrs Potter showed them the cages.

'I hope you're lucky, my dear. There were two new dogs this morning – a white poodle and a brown terrier.'

'I hope that it's Terry!' Sharon thought and looked at her mother.

The dogs in the first cage jumped when they saw Sharon. They were happy that somebody was visiting them. They barked a lot. Are you my new owner? they asked with their sad eyes.

The terrier was in the second cage. It didn't jump at Sharon. It was asleep. It had a bloody nose. It looked like Terry, but it wasn't Terry. Sharon stayed in front of the cage and looked at the poor dog.

'How terrible! I'd like to help, but I can't,' Sharon said when she felt her mother's arm around her.

'I'm so sorry. I'm so sorry, my dear,' Mrs Potter said. 'What a pity!'

‘It’s time to go home, Sharon,’ Mrs Payne said.

‘We have a nice hamster ... Perhaps ...’

‘No, thank you, Mrs Potter. You’re very kind. We have a dog and we’re going to find him.’

‘Why don’t you ask the police? Sometimes people take animals to the police station,’ Mrs Potter said.

Sharon looked at her mother. ‘Why not? Let’s go to the police station, Mum.’

On the way to the police station Sharon thought of the terrier in Mrs Potter’s cage.

CHAPTER 7

'Here's the whisky bottle. It was in your pocket, Larry!' a police officer said.

What was Larry doing at the police station? And what was Asif doing here? Everybody in Chester knew Larry. He was a homeless old man who liked whisky.

'It isn't the first time, Larry. It isn't funny. If you want to drink, you have to pay for the bottle.' The officer was angry, but Larry wasn't listening.

Poor Larry! Sharon liked the old man. She thought about the terrier in Mrs Potter's cage.

The police officer took Larry away.

'What are they going to do with Larry? Put him in a cage like the dogs at the animal home? I must ask Asif this evening,' Sharon thought.

'Hallo, I'm Sergeant Simpson. What can I do for you two?' asked a young policewoman.

Mrs Payne and Sharon told Terry's story again.

'Mmh,' Sergeant Simpson said after a long time. 'Your dog – what's his name?'

'Terry.'

'What does Terry look like, Sharon?'

Sharon described Terry.

'That's very good, Sharon. You can describe things very well,' Sergeant Simpson smiled. Sharon felt good. It wasn't really a problem for a 'detective' like her.

'But I'm sorry, Sharon. I can't help you. I don't know where your dog is. Somebody brought a dog to the police station two days ago, but yesterday and today there was nothing.'

Mrs Payne put her arm around her daughter.

'But you must find him! You must find him!' Now there were tears in Sharon's eyes. 'Please! Please!'

'Well, I can see you really love your dog,' Sergeant Simpson said. 'But our police officers are very busy. And it isn't easy to find a dog. But your story is interesting, Sharon.'

'Why, Sergeant Simpson?'

'Well, last week there were three dog owners with the same story. All the dogs were in the park with their owners when they disappeared. We have information from the police in Liverpool that there are some animal hunters from Liverpool in Chester.'

'Animal hunters? What do they do?' Sharon asked.

'Well, these people are bad, Sharon. They find stray dogs and cats and put them in cages.'

‘What? Dogs and cats? Why? Why, Sergeant Simpson?’ Sharon was worried.

‘Well, they get money for the cats and dogs. They sell them to laboratories. The laboratories need cats, dogs, mice, rabbits and other animals for experiments.’

‘Experiments? What do you mean?’

Sergeant Simpson looked at Mrs Payne. Sharon’s face was red. She was angry. There were more tears in her eyes now.

‘Well, companies need experiments for new medicines. They have to know that the medicine is good. Then people can buy the medicine,’ Sergeant Simpson explained. ‘It’s very sad for the animals, but we need medicine.’

‘But they stole my dog. He’s not a stray dog,’ Sharon cried.

‘Sharon, please,’ Mrs Payne said. ‘Don’t worry.’

Sharon was frightened.

‘Your mother is right,’ Sergeant Simpson said. ‘Don’t worry. Lots of dogs run away and come back to their owners.’

Sharon didn’t answer. She thought about Sergeant Simpson’s words: animal hunters – money – experiments – don’t worry – don’t worry.

When she left the police station she saw a poster near the door. Sharon read ‘WANTED’. Sharon didn’t like the faces on the poster. Larry wasn’t like them. Sharon thought of her favourite TV programme ‘TV Police Time’. Every Sunday evening she felt like one of the police officers. And she was better than them – on the sofa in front of the TV, of course. She looked at the faces again. Are these the faces of the animal hunters?

CHAPTER 8

'There's somebody at the door, Sharon. Please go and see who's there,' Mrs Payne said. She was making lunch in the kitchen. Sharon was in the living-room.

'I'm busy,' Sharon grumbled. 'I'm reading an interesting book about animal experiments.'

'Sharon, please! There's somebody at the door!'

'OK, Mum.'

'Who is it, Sharon?'

'It's Asif and Dave. Come in, boys.'

'Is Terry back?' Dave asked. He looked into Sharon's eyes and knew the answer.

'Does Terry have a telephone number on his collar?' Asif asked.

'Terry's collar broke last week. He has a new collar now. But it doesn't have our telephone number,' Sharon said.

'Oh no!'

'I'm so sorry for you,' Dave said. 'Sometimes Boris goes away, too. One night – two nights. But it's different with cats. They like to be free. Dogs like to be with their families all the time.'

Sharon, Dave and Asif went into the kitchen. They drank some milk and ate some biscuits.

'Last week I watched a report about animal hunters on TV,' Dave said. 'They're terrible. I'm worried about Boris. Perhaps one night they're going to take him, too.'

'Sharon, you can't sit at home and wait for Terry! Let's do

something!' Asif said. 'Let's make posters. Lots of posters. Everybody in Chester must know that we're looking for Terry.'

'You're right, Asif,' Sharon said.

'Let's put them on trees and in shop windows,' Dave said.

'I'm going to put three posters in our shop window,' Asif said. Everybody laughed.

'It's good to have friends,' Sharon thought.

'Let's start now,' she said. 'In my bedroom there's a big photo of Terry.'

An hour later they finished the poster.

'I like it,' Dave said.

'It's great,' Sharon said.

'How many copies do we need?' Asif asked.

'Well, I have enough pocket-money for 40 copies at Turner's Copy Shop.'

'Are you copying your maths homework for your friends, Sharon?' Mr Turner asked.

Sharon told him about Terry and the posters.

'That's a great idea. Can I have a poster for my shop window?'

'Of course!' Sharon smiled.

Sharon, Dave and Asif walked through Chester.

'Here are some posters for you, Dave, and here are some for you, Asif. It's three o'clock now,' Sharon said. 'Let's meet in two hours.'

When Asif arrived at The Coffee Cup café, it was nearly five o'clock. Asif saw Sharon and Dave in the café.

'Are you OK, Asif?' Dave asked.

'Well, I'm as tired as a football after a Manchester United match. But I'm happy. Some of my posters are on trees in the park. Some of them are in the streets around the park. I'm sure that somebody can help us.'

'Good idea, Asif,' Sharon said.

'I'm happy, too. All the shopkeepers were friendly,' Dave explained. 'They all want to help us.'

'Well, I'm sure Terry is the talk of the town tonight.' Sharon laughed. 'Listen, boys! I have some news. I met one of our neighbours, Mrs Austin, at the library. Her poodle Cindy is also missing. Yesterday she was in the ...'

'...in the park?'

'You're right, Asif. In the park.'

'First it's Terry, then it's Cindy. What's going on?' Dave asked.

'We must learn more about these animal hunters,' Asif said. 'This is a real holiday adventure.'

CHAPTER 9

'Would you like another sausage, Sharon?'

'No, thank you, Dad. I'm not really hungry. I feel terrible.'

'But you must eat ...'

'Is that the phone?'

'Yes,' Mr Payne said. 'Let me go and see who it is.'

Sharon thought about all the posters in town. There was a photo of Terry here, and there was a photo of Terry there. It wasn't easy to walk through the streets. Sharon saw Terry everywhere. But Terry was not at home.

'Please say the name again, Mrs Applebee. ... Harald Jones – Removals ... OK, Mrs Applebee ... From Liverpool ... You're not sure ... Oh, I see. It was too dark ... The rain ... Yes, I understand ... That's a great help, Mrs Applebee. Thank you very much ... Good-bye.'

Sharon was worried.

'What's the matter, Dad?'

'Mrs Applebee has some information for us,' Mr Payne said. 'She saw one of your posters in the park. She lives near the north gate.'

'Go on, Dad.'

'Mrs Applebee doesn't know where Terry is. But last Sunday she saw a van with the name 'Harald Jones – Removals' on it. Mrs Applebee thinks it's a firm in Liverpool. She isn't sure, but she is sure about one thing.'

'What's that, Dad?' Sharon asked.

'Mrs Applebee knows all her neighbours, and nobody moved house in her street last Sunday.'

Everybody was surprised.

'We have a telephone directory for Liverpool. Grandma gave us one last year. Do you remember?' Luke said.

'Good idea. There's another young detective in our family,' Mr Payne smiled at Luke.

'Jackson ... Jenkins ... Jones,' Sharon read. She was worried again. 'There are so many people with the name

'Jones' ... Chris ... Gavin ... Harald ... Here it is ... Harald Jones ... Harald Jones – Removals. His firm is in Queen's Street.'

'Mrs Applebee was right. The firm is in Liverpool,' Mrs Payne said.

'Tomorrow is Saturday. I'm not working, so we can go to Liverpool tomorrow,' Mr Payne said.

'Great. I'm very hungry now. Can I have a sausage, Mum?' Sharon asked.

Sharon felt much better now.

CHAPTER 10

'There are five cans of lemonade and some sandwiches in the picnic bag. It's going to be hot again today.'

'OK, Mum. Don't worry.'

A few minutes later Mr Payne's old car was on the motorway. Mr Payne, Sharon, Luke, Kevin, Asif and Dave were driving to Liverpool. 'It's nice in the country,' Sharon thought. The fields and the trees were green and the birds were singing. It was early in the morning, and the villages were still asleep.

'Manchester United is playing this afternoon in Liverpool. I'd like to watch the match. Perhaps we ...'

'Oh Asif! We're in Liverpool because we have to find Terry – not because we want to watch a football match,' Sharon said.

Asif grumbled.

'I'm hungry,' Dave said.

'Oh Dave! You're always hungry. You had breakfast two hours ago.'

'A good detective needs a second breakfast,' Asif said.

Everybody laughed.

'What are we going to do with the animal hunters if we find them?' Luke asked.

'We're going to phone the police,' Dave said.

'No, we're going to throw them into the dungeon of an old castle,' Asif said. 'With only water and spiders!'

They all laughed again.

'I love your mum's sandwiches, Sharon!' Dave smiled and ate another cheese and tomato sandwich.

An hour later the five detectives were in Liverpool. They couldn't find Queen's Street.

'Please, Sharon, look at the map again,' Mr Payne said.

'You have to drive along Albert Road, then turn left into Station Road. Then turn left again,' Sharon said.

It was summer, but this part of Liverpool was not very nice. There were lots of dark streets. From some of the houses you could hear loud music. It wasn't very friendly. Buckingham Palace wasn't in Queen's Street. There was lots of rubbish in this street. Some of the windows of the houses were broken. There was nobody in the street.

'Gosh, it's terrible here,' Dave said.

'I'm glad we don't live here,' said Sharon.

'There they are! There they are!' Asif suddenly shouted.

'Who, Asif? Who?'

'There they are!'

Then everybody saw the flags – lots of red and white flags. There was a group of United fans at the end of the street. They were walking towards the football stadium.

'The match against Liverpool,' Asif explained. 'It's going to start soon.'

Everybody looked at Asif. 'What's the matter?' he thought. Then Asif was quiet.

'Stop, Dad! Here it is. Number 84.'

Harald Jones' firm was behind a high wall. There was no name on it – only the number.

'Harald Jones doesn't like visitors,' Sharon thought.

Was Terry here?

'Everything is very old here,' Dave said. 'The gate is locked, but here's a hole.'

'What can you see?' Sharon asked.

'I can see a building and … a shed … a large shed.'

'A large shed. That's interesting,' Sharon thought. 'A shed is a good place to hide animals.'

'Listen!' Mr Payne said. 'Let's go back to the car and watch the gate.'

'Good idea, Dad,' Luke said. 'Like real detectives.'

'Here's some money, Dave,' Mr Payne said. 'There's a small shop at the end of the street. Go and buy five ice-creams there.'

CHAPTER 11

'Moore has the ball. He's in front of the United goal now – and he scores. Moore scores. It's 2:1 for Liverpool.'

Asif was angry with the reporter on the radio, but his ice-cream was OK.

'I'm going to phone Sergeant Simpson,' Sharon said. 'Perhaps she can help us.'

'We can tell her about our trip to Liverpool when we're back in Chester,' Mr Payne said.

'OK, Dad.'

Then they waited.

'Goal! Goal!' the reporter on the radio shouted five minutes later. 'It's a goal for United.'

'Hooray!' Asif shouted.

Then they waited again.

'Let's drive back to Chester, Sharon,' Mr Payne said after three hours. 'There's nobody here. It's very quiet.'

'Too quiet,' Luke answered. 'But you're right, Dad.'

'Wait a minute,' Sharon said. 'There's a car rental firm over there. Perhaps they know Harald Jones. Perhaps they have some information about this man.'

'Yes, let's go and ask,' the others said.

Mr Payne and the children crossed a big car park. They saw some cars and some caravans. And Sharon counted five vans. In a small building at the end of the car park they saw a young woman behind a table. There was a sign in front of her. SHIRLEY HOLMES – Sharon read. But the woman didn't look like Sherlock Holmes' sister.

'Hallo, do you want to hire one of our vans?' Miss Holmes asked. She had chewing gum in her mouth.

Mr Payne was surprised.

'We can give you a big van for you and all your children!' Miss Holmes smiled.

There were lots of maps, timetables and lists on the wall behind her.

'Oh ... well ... I understand, but you're wrong, Miss Holmes. We don't want a van, we want ...,' Mr Payne said.

'You can hire a caravan for a weekend trip. It's only £60. We have great prices, Sir,' Miss Holmes smiled again.

'Well ... thank you, Miss Holmes ... but what we need is information,' Mr Payne said.

Suddenly the young woman looked bored. Then all the children told Terry's story again.

'That's a sad story.' Miss Holmes put her chewing gum under the table. 'I have a dog, too. I'm really sorry, but I can't help you. This is a car rental firm, not a dog rental firm.'

'What do you know about Harald Jones and his firm?'

'What does he have in his shed?'

'What's in Harald Jones' van?'

Miss Holmes laughed.

'Just a minute! That's a lot of questions, kids! I'm sorry. I can't give you any information.'

'Please ... please, Miss Holmes!' the children said. 'Think of your own little dog!'

'OK. You win,' Miss Holmes said. 'But don't record this on video.'

Everybody laughed.

'What is in Harald Jones' van? Well, I hope that there are cupboards, tables and beds in it. But I'm not so sure.'

The children listened carefully.

'Well, the neighbours here don't like Mr Jones. He's an unfriendly man. People say that he doesn't have much work. I don't think that he has many customers. I see the van only twice a week. Perhaps Mr Jones has...'

'... another job?' Sharon asked.

Miss Holmes nodded her head.

'When does the van leave this place?' Luke asked.

'Well, the van always leaves on Friday and comes back on Tuesday.'

'Tuesday,' Asif said. 'Today is Saturday. That's why everything is quiet over there.'

'Thank you very much, Miss Homes,' Mr Payne said. 'You're a great help.'

'But please remember...'

'What?'

'Well, I'm not Sherlock Holmes' sister and you aren't Sherlock Holmes.'

Everybody laughed.

On their way to the motorway Mr Payne and the children saw lots of United fans. The match was over. The children didn't talk. Terry wasn't with them. But there was hope now.

And Asif was happy – United won 3:2.

CHAPTER 12

'Hallo, Mr Ahmed.'

'Oh, hallo, Sharon. How are you?'

'Well, holidays are better than lessons, but I miss Terry. He disappeared eight days ago and I'm so worried.'

'It's really terrible, Sharon. But I have the new *Shout* for you – just like every Monday.'

'Great, Mr Ahmed … £1.30 … Here you are.'

'Thank you, Sharon.'

Sharon walked down Elm Road and looked at her favourite magazine. She liked the posters and the problem letters best. What's this? LABORATORY ANIMALS NEED YOUR HELP, Sharon read. It was a report about ANIMAL HELP. ANIMAL HELP was against animal experiments. Sharon was interested. 'But what can I do?' she thought. Lots of animals die in laboratory experiments, Sharon read. We speak for them. Animal experiments are wrong. What can you do in your own life? Come to ANIMAL HELP and organise your own youth club in your town. Then open the eyes of other people.

'That's a great idea,' Sharon thought. 'I'm going to be a member.' Sharon felt good. 'I must talk to mum and dad about ANIMAL HELP this evening.'

'What about hamburgers and hot dogs?' Kevin asked.

'Kevin, don't you understand?' Sharon was angry. 'We don't need to eat meat.'

The Paynes were having tea. There weren't any sausages on Sharon's plate.

'Animals are my friends. I don't eat my friends, Kevin.'

'Well, I don't think you can speak for everybody, Sharon,' Mrs Payne said. 'It isn't as easy as you think. Look at your leather shoes, Sharon!'

'They're going to be my last, Mum,' Sharon said.

'I like meat, too,' Mr Payne said. 'We don't use animals only for food. We use them in experiments for cosmetics, too. We don't need to buy those things. Let's buy natural products.'

'That's a good idea, George,' Mrs Payne said.

'That's great, Mum and Dad,' Sharon said. 'You're the first members in my ANIMAL HELP YOUTH CLUB.'

'What a surprise! I'm young again!' Mrs Payne smiled.

'I have a surprise for you, too, Sharon,' Mr Payne said. 'I'm going to Liverpool tomorrow morning. You, Luke, Asif and Dave can come with me. We're going to visit the Jones' building again.'

'Tomorrow – that's Tuesday!' Detective Sharon was happy.

'Can I have another sausage, Mum?' Kevin asked.

CHAPTER 13

'That's a good idea, Mr Payne,' Asif said and pointed at the ladder in Mr Payne's old car. The car was in Queen's Street again. It was opposite Harald Jones' firm.

'I have my old binoculars with me,' Mr Payne said.

'You're a real detective, Dad!' Sharon said. Mr Payne smiled.

From the ladder Sharon could see over the wall. She looked through the binoculars. There was the shed. Everything was quiet.

'Over there!' Sharon shouted.

'What can you see?'

'There are some empty cages.'

'I think this is the right address,' Mr Payne said. 'Let's go back to the car and wait there.'

Sharon was worried. It was six o'clock, but nothing was happening.

'Somebody is opening the gate,' Asif suddenly shouted. Asif was right. They saw a young man. He was wearing blue jeans and a green pullover. He had a mobile phone with him.

'I'm sure that the other animal hunters phoned him. That's why he is opening the gate,' Sharon said. 'Some new dogs and cats are going to arrive soon.'

'I don't feel OK,' Dave said. 'This is too much for me!'

'Shhh, Dave!'

Asif looked through the binoculars.

'A van is coming!' he said. He was worried, too. 'I can see it at the end of the street. There's a name on it.'

'Can you read the name?' Sharon asked.

'It's ... Harald ... Jones ... Removals.'

The black van drove past the open gate. At that moment Sharon got out of her father's car. She ran behind the black

van. The driver of the van and the young man at the gate didn't see her. Mr Payne and the boys were surprised. They wanted to shout Sharon's name, but it was too late. The young man closed the gate.

The van stopped in front of the shed. Sharon hid behind the empty cages. The driver opened the van. Then Sharon saw the first cage. There was a dog in it. The young man took the cage into the shed. Then he came back and took the second cage. Soon all of the cages were in the shed. Sharon counted ten cages.

Then Sharon ran into the shed, too. The two men were talking. What were they saying? They were in front of the other cages now. Dogs were barking. Lots of dogs. They were crying, 'Help! Help us!' Sharon ran behind an old cupboard. From here she could see all the cages. There were some terriers, too. Terry, are you here? Terry, where are you?

'What are you doing here?'

Sharon was surprised. The young man was behind her. He was angry.

'Come with me!' he said. He took her by the arm. Sharon was frightened. She wanted to run away, but the young man was stronger than Sharon.

'Police! Hands up!'

Sharon was surprised again. She saw three police officers.

'Sharon, are you all right?' a young police officer asked.

'Yes, I am, but ...'

'Well, your father told Sergeant Simpson on Saturday evening about Mrs Applebee and your trip to Liverpool. Sergeant Simpson phoned us and told us about Harald Jones' firm. On Sunday we sent a police car here and today the van finally arrived with the animals.'

Then Sharon saw her father, Luke, Asif and Dave.

'Are you OK, Sharon?'

'Yes, I am, Dad,' Sharon answered. 'This is like "TV Police Time".'

'You're right, Sharon,' the police officer said. 'It is 'police time' – but it's not on TV!'

'May I see if Terry is here?' Sharon asked.

'Of course.'

The children ran to the cages.

'Terry? Terry – are you here?'

'Perhaps he's already in a laboratory,' Sharon thought. Now she was near the last cages.

'Terry! Terry! There you are! Don't you remember me? It's me, Sharon! I'm so happy, Terry! You're back!'

Terry was very thin, and his eyes were tired.

'There's blood around his nose, but I think he's OK,' Dave said.

'I'm going to phone the animal home,' the police officer said. 'They can help the animals. We have to find all the owners. We're going to arrest the two men here, but we have to find Mr Jones. He's not here.'

Sharon opened the cage and put her arms around Terry. She was so happy.

'Let's go home, Terry!'

CHAPTER 14

'Woof! Woof!'

Sharon was playing with Terry in her bedroom. They were having fun. Terry liked his new bone. It was a present from Sharon.

'Sharon! Where are you? Your friends are coming soon,' shouted Mrs Payne from the kitchen.

Sharon was wearing her new blue jeans and a new T-shirt. There was a picture of Terry on it with the name ANIMAL HELP under it. Sharon looked at the *Chester Times* on her bed. 'Police Arrest Three Animal Hunters. Young Girl from Chester Helps Police.' Next to the report there was a photo of Sharon. Sharon smiled. She felt good.

'Mrs Kelly, Asif and Dave are here. Please come and say hallo, Sharon,' Mrs Payne shouted.

'Hallo, Mrs Kelly! Hi, Asif and Dave! The party is in our office,' Sharon said when she went into the kitchen.

'In our office?' Asif asked.

'Yes, our ANIMAL HELP YOUTH CLUB office. We can use the shed in the garden. Mum and dad say it's OK. Dad's going to give us his old computer and printer. We have some badges and posters from ANIMAL HELP and lots of brochures, of course. We also have some cosmetics that aren't animal-tested. And we can sell some natural products.'

'It's just like our shop,' Asif laughed.

'I'm going to buy something every week,' Mrs Kelly was very interested.

ANIMAL HELP
YOUTH CLUB
CHESTER
Animal
Help

'There are some sandwiches and drinks in Sharon's office,' Mrs Payne said.

There were lots of people in the garden now. Mrs Brown, Sharon's teacher, was there, too. She brought a poster with a rabbit on it.

'It looks like Dave,' Sharon said. 'I'm going to put it on our office door.'

'Here's another thing for the office door,' Mr Payne said.

'Oh, Dad. What is it? It's in a box! It looks like a surprise,' Sharon shouted. Sharon opened the box. There was a metal sign in it with the name ANIMAL HELP YOUTH CLUB CHESTER.

'That's great, Dad! Thank you!' She gave her dad a big hug.

'We now have ten members,' Luke said and showed Sharon a list with lots of names. Sharon was happy.

'Luke, please tell them that we're going to meet next Monday evening in our office. We're going to talk about our first project.'

'Your first project?' Mr Kelly asked.

'Yes, we're going to organise a stall in front of the town hall,' Sharon explained. 'We're going to sell brochures, badges and posters. And we're going to sell our products, too.'

'That's a good idea,' Mr Kelly said. 'I'm going to bring drinks and sandwiches. "Kelly's Kitchen" for ANIMAL HELP!'

Everybody laughed.

'It's not easy to find you, Detective Sharon.'

Sharon turned round. It was Sergeant Simpson.

'What a surprise, Sergeant Simpson. What are you doing here?'

'Well, I heard about your club. I think it's a good idea. And I have a present from the police officers and from me,'

Sergeant Simpson said. 'You helped the police a lot, Sharon! We arrested Mr Jones and his two friends. Lots of people now have their pets back and are very happy. So we wanted to give you a present, too. Would you like to sit in a police car, watch our officers and help them with their work for one day?'

'That's great. I can't wait. May I turn on the blue light, too, Sergeant Simpson?'

'Of course, Sharon.'

'But don't forget that Sharon has to wear handcuffs, Sergeant Simpson,' Mr Payne said. They all laughed.

'Sandwiches and drinks for everybody,' Mrs Payne shouted.

'I'm so hungry,' Dave said.

'Oh Dave! Why don't you join a cooking club?' Sharon laughed. Then they saw Kevin and Terry. Kevin was eating a sandwich, and Terry was playing with his new bone.

'I like your party, Sharon!' Kevin said.

'Thank you.'

'Can I have a picnic tomorrow, too? With Luke and Terry in the park?'

ARE YOU A GOOD 'STORY DETECTIVE'?

A Lots of people helped Sharon with her first case. Find the right people:

1. *She saw Harald Jones' van near Chester Park.* (Chapter 9)
2. *He drove the young detectives to Liverpool on Saturday and again on Tuesday.* (Chapters 10 and 13)
3. *He put a poster in his shop window.* (Chapter 8)
4. *She told Liverpool Police about Harald Jones' firm.* (Chapter 13)
5. *She told the detectives when Harald Jones' van came and went.* (Chapter 11)
6. *He had the idea with the posters, and he put lots of them on the trees in Chester Park.* (Chapter 8)
7. *She told Sharon that people sometimes take stray animals to the police.* (Chapter 6)
8. *They arrested the animal hunters.* (Chapter 13)
9. *She made super sandwiches for the detectives.* (Chapter 10)

B Find the missing words. Put the letters in boxes into the right order. They give you a word from the text.

1. *Luke and Kevin went to Chester Park for a* _ _ _ _ ❐ _.
2. *Terry was in a cage in* _ _ ❐ _ _ _ _ _ _.
3. *Animals are Sharon's friends, so she doesn't eat* _ ❐ _ _.
4. *Terry's favourite place is under a big* _ _ _ _ ❐ _ _ _ _.

5. *Mr Ahmed put the newspaper in Terry's _ _ _ _ □ _ _ _ _ _ .*
6. *There are lots of animal experiments before companies can sell new _ _ _ _ □ _ _ _ .*
7. *Terry disappeared in the park. Was it Luke's _ _ _ _ □ ?*
8. *Mr Payne and the children travelled to Liverpool again on _ _ □ _ _ _ _ _ .*
9. *In the first night without Terry Sharon had bad □ _ _ _ _ _ _ .*

C A secret message from Sharon to Sergeant Simpson. Do you know what the message is?

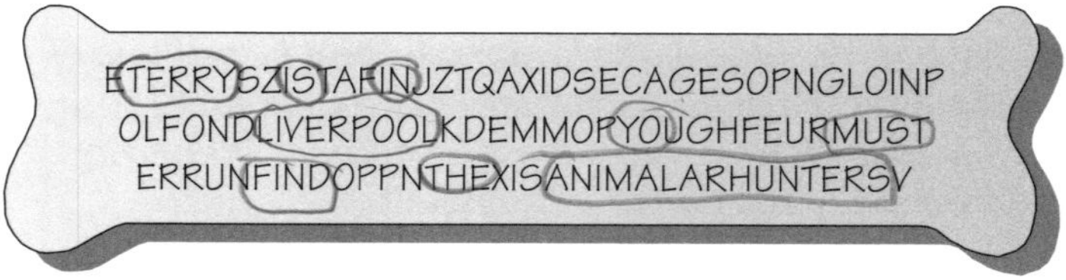

D Find 14 words from 14 chapters. Put them in the right order. They are an ANIMAL HELP slogan.

Chapter 1: Where is the newspaper? On Terry's plastic bag or in Terry's plastic bag?

Chapter 2: Find the missing word: *A game with Boris … then a walk to the park!*

Chapter 3: What's the missing word? Luke buys too … hamburgers with his pocket-money, so he doesn't have any money for trainers.

Chapter 4: *There were … many people, … many dogs, … many trees and … many bushes in the park.* Find the missing word.

Chapter 5: One word is missing: *The Paynes' car was … a boat on the River Mersey.*

Chapter 6: Mrs Potter has one of them. You need the plural.
Chapter 7: Companies need to do them before they can sell a new medicine.
Chapter 8: This animal likes to be free. You need the plural.
Chapter 9: One word is missing: Sharon isn't hungry, because she feels …
Chapter 10: What can one hide in a large shed?
Chapter 11: You can't hire them at a car rental.
Chapter 12: Find the missing word: *Lots of animals … in laboratory experiments*.
Chapter 13: What's the missing word? Terry wasn't in a … – he was still in a cage in the shed.
Chapter 14: It's on Mrs Brown's poster. You need the plural.

E Make the poster that Sharon, Asif and Dave put on trees and shop-windows in Chester. You can draw a picture of Terry, too.

F Write the report about Sharon's first case in the *Chester Times*. Find a headline, too.

G Write the story from Terry's point of view.

H ANIMAL HELP YOUTH CLUB CHESTER has a stall in front of Chester's town hall.
Work with your partners and write some dialogues between members of the youth club and other people. Then act the scene. You can make badges with slogans *(Leather jackets? Don't buy them!; Don't let our friends die!; Against animal experiments)* and posters, too.

I When Sharon came back from Liverpool she phoned her Grandma and told her Terry's story. Work with a partner and write the dialogue. Then act the scene.

J Write to ANIMAL AID in England. They're against animal experiments. Ask for a free leaflet package. Work with your partners and make an information wall. Do interviews with students and teachers, write short reports, make posters with slogans, show pictures and collages, etc.

Animal Aid
The Old Chapel
Bradford St
Tonbridge
Kent TN9 1AW
England

They also have a website at: http://www.animalaid.org.uk.

VOCABULARY

Abbreviations

n = noun
s.p.f. = simple past form
sth. = something
v = verb

A

against [ə'genst] gegen
animal-tested ['ænıml testıd] an Tieren / im Tierversuch getestet
another [ə'nʌðə] noch ein(e)
around [ə'raʊnd] um; um ... herum
arrest (v) [ə'rest] verhaften
ate [eıt]: s.p.f. of **eat** essen

B

bad [bæd] schlecht
bark (n) [bɑ:k] Bellen
barked [bɑ:kt]: s.p.f. of **bark** (v) [bɑ:k] bellen
bin [bın] Mülleimer
binoculars [bı'nɒkjələz] Fernglas
blanket ['blæŋkıt] Decke
bloody ['blʌdi] blutig
bone [bəʊn] Knochen
brought [brɔ:t]: s.p.f. of **bring** [brıŋ] (mit)bringen
building ['bıldıŋ] Gebäude

C

café ['kæfeı] Café
car rental firm ['kɑ: rentl fɜ:m] Mietwagenverleih
carefully ['keəfəli] aufmerksam
cartoon [kɑ:'tu:n] Zeichentrickfilm
case [keıs] Fall
champion ['tʃæmpiən] Meister
chewing gum ['tʃu:ıŋ gʌm] Kaugummi
clever ['klevə] klug, schlau
clock [klɒk] Uhr
collar ['kɒlə] Halsband
company ['kʌmpəni] Firma
cooking club ['kʊkıŋ klʌb] Kochclub
copy (n) ['kɒpi] Kopie
copy (v) ['kɒpi] kopieren
cosmetics [kɒz'metıkz] Kosmetikartikel, Kosmetika

D

dear (n) [dıə] Liebe(r)
described: s.p.f. of **describe** [dı'skraıb] beschreiben
die [daı] sterben

disappeared: s.p.f. of **disappear** [dɪsə'pɪə] verschwinden
drank [dræŋk]: s.p.f. of **drink** [drɪŋk] trinken
dream (n) ['dri:m] Traum
dungeon ['dʌndʒən] Verlies, Kerker

E
empty ['empti] leer
end (n) [end] Ende
experiment [ɪk'sperɪmənt] Experiment, Versuch
eye [aɪ] Auge

F
face [feɪs] Gesicht
fast [fɑ:st] schnell
it's our/your fault [fɔ:lt] es ist unsere/deine Schuld
finally ['faɪnəli] endlich
forever [fər'evə] ewig
front door [frʌnt 'dɔ:] Haustür

G
gate [geɪt] Tor
goal [gəʊl] Tor
gosh! [gɒʃ] Mensch!
got in: s.p.f. of **get in** einsteigen
got out of: s.p.f. of **get out of** aussteigen

H
handcuffs ['hændkʌfs] Handschellen
hands up! Hände hoch!
heard [herd]: s.p.f. of **hear** [hɪə] hören
help (n) [help] Hilfe
hid [hɪd]: s.p.f. of **hide** [haɪd] verstecken
play hide-and-seek [haɪdən'si:k] Verstecken spielen
hole [həʊl] Loch
homeless ['həʊmləs] obdachlos
hooray [hu'reɪ] hurra
hope (n) [həʊp] Hoffnung
hot [hɒt] heiß
hug [hʌg] Umarmung
hunter [hʌntə] Jäger/in, Fänger/in

I
if [ɪf] wenn, falls

J
joke [dʒəʊk] Witz
just ['dʒʌst] genau

K
kind [kaɪnd] freundlich, hilfsbereit
knew [nju:]: s.p.f. of **know** [nəʊ] kennen

L
laboratory [lə'bɒrətr] Labor
ladder ['lædə] Leiter
lake [leɪk] See
lazy ['leɪzi] faul (schläfrig, müde)
leather shoes ['leðə 'ʃu:z] Lederschuhe
lightning ['laɪtnɪŋ] Blitz
like wie; mögen, gern haben
locked [lɒkt] verschlossen
loud [laʊd] laut
love (v) [lʌv] lieben, gern haben
luck [lʌk] Glück

M
main [meɪn] Haupt-
what do you mean? [mi:n] was wollen Sie damit sagen?
medicine ['medsn] Medikament
member ['membə] Mitglied
met [met]: s.p.f. of **meet** treffen
miaow [mi'aʊ] miauen
missing ['mɪsɪŋ] weg, verschwunden
mobile phone ['məʊbaɪl 'fəʊn] Handy, Mobiltelefon
monster ['mɒnstə] Monster, Ungeheuer

motorway ['məʊtəweɪ] Autobahn
moved house: s.p.f. of **move house** [mu:v] umziehen

N

natural products ['nætʃrəl 'prɒdʌkts] Naturprodukte
nearly ['nɪəli] fast
news [nju:z] Nachrichten, Neuigkeiten
nod one's head [nɒd] mit dem Kopf nicken
noise [nɔɪz] Geräusch
nose [nəʊz] Nase
not even [nɒt 'i:vən] nicht einmal

O

open (v) ['əʊpən] öffnen
owner ['əʊnə] Besitzer(in)

P

picnic ['pɪknɪk] Picknick
pocket ['pɒkɪt] Tasche
pointed (at): s.p.f. of **point (at)** [pɔɪnt] zeigen (auf)
poodle ['pu:dl] Pudel
poor [pʊə] arm
poured [pɔ:d]: s.p.f. of **pour** [pɔ:] gießen
printer ['prɪntə] Drucker

R

rain (v) [reɪn] regnen
it's raining cats and dogs ['reɪnɪŋ] Es regnet Bindfäden
raindrop ['reɪndrɒp] Regentropfen
ran [ræn]: s.p.f. of **run** laufen, rennen
ran down: s.p.f. of **run down** hinunterlaufen
read [red]: s.p.f. of **read** [ri:d] lesen
ready ['redi] fertig
real ['ri:əl] echt
removal van [rɪ'mu:vl væn] Umzugswagen
removals [rɪ'mu:vlz] Umzüge
run away weglaufen

S

score [skɔ:] ein Tor schießen
sent: s.p.f. of **send** [send] schicken
Sergeant ['sɑ:dʒənt] Wachtmeister(in)
shaving foam ['ʃeɪvɪŋ fəʊm] Rasierschaum
shed [ʃed] Schuppen
shouted: s.p.f. of **shout** [ʃaʊt] rufen
smiled: s.p.f. of **smile** [smaɪl] lächeln
sofa ['səʊfə] Sofa
stadium ['steɪdiəm] Stadion
still [stɪl] noch
stole [stəʊl]: s.p.f. of **steal** [sti:l] stehlen
stray ['streɪ] streunend, herrenlos
stroked: s.p.f. of **stroke** [strəʊk] streicheln
stronger [strɒŋgə] stärker
swimming pool ['swɪmɪŋ pu:l] Schwimmbad

T

he's the talk of the town er ist das Gesprächsthema Nummer 1 in der Stadt
tear [tɪə] Träne
telephone directory ['telɪfəʊn dərektəri] Telefonbuch
terrier ['teriə] Terrier
thin [θɪn] dünn, mager
throw [θrəʊ] werfen
thunderclap ['θʌndəklæp] Donnerschlag
thunderstorm ['θʌndəstɔ:m] Gewitter
turn round [tɜ:n 'raʊnd] sich umdrehen

towards [tə'wɔ:dz] zum, auf … zu
trainer ['treɪnə] Sportschuh, Turnschuh
twice [twaɪs] zweimal

U
use (v) [ju:z] benutzen, verwenden

W
walk (n) [wɔ:k] Spaziergang
wall [wɔ:l] Mauer
want (v) ['wɒnt] wollen
want to do sth. ['wɒnt] etwas tun wollen
'wanted' ['wɒntɪd] 'gesucht'
water (v) ['wɔ:tə] gießen
whisky ['wɪski] Whisky
worried ['wʌri:d] besorgt